Presented To:

Presented By:

Date:

from a
Daughter's
Heart
to her
Mom

NELSON BOOKS
A Division of Thomas Nelson Publishers
Since 1798

www.thomasnelson.com

Published in Nashville, Tennessee, by Thomas Nelson, Inc.

Nelson Books titles may be purchased in bulk for educational, business, fund-raising, or sales promotional use. For information, please e-mail SpecialMarkets@ThomasNelson.com.

Scripture quotations noted NKJV are from The New King James Version®. Copyright © 1979, 1980, 1982 by Thomas Nelson, Inc. Used by permission. All rights reserved.

Scripture quotations noted GNT are from the Good News Translation, Second Edition, copyright © 1992 by American Bible Society. Used by permission. All rights reserved.

Scripture quotations noted MSG are from *The Message*. Copyright © by Eugene H. Peterson 1993, 1994, 1995. Used by permission of NavPress Publishing Group.

Scripture quotations noted NCV are from The Holy Bible, New Century Version, copyright © 1987, 1988, 1991 by Word Publishing, a division of Thomas Nelson, Inc. All rights reserved. Used by permission.

Scripture quotations noted NIV are from the Holy Bible: New International Version®. Copyright © 1973, 1978, 1984 by International Bible Society. Used by permission of Zondervan Publishing House. All rights reserved.

Scripture quotations noted NLT are from the *Holy Bible*, New Living Translation, copyright © 1996. Used by permission of Tyndale House Publishers, Inc., Wheaton, Illinois 60189. All rights reserved.

Scripture quotations noted NRSV are from The New Revised Standard Version of the Bible. Copyright © 1989 by the Division of Christian Education of the National Council of the Churches of Christ in the U.S.A. All rights reserved.

Managing Editor: Lila Empson
Associate Editor: Kyle L. Olund
Manuscript: Heather Ivester
Design: Whisner Design Group, Tulsa, Oklahoma

Library of Congress Cataloging-in-Publication Data

From a daughter's heart to her mom : 50 reflections on living well.
    p. cm.
  ISBN 0-7852-1432-1 (hardcover)
  1. Mothers--Prayer-books and devotions--English. 2. Christian women--Prayer-books and devotions--English. 3. Mothers and daughters--Religious aspects--Christianity--Meditations. 4. Christian life--Meditations. I. Thomas Nelson Publishers.
  BV4847.F76 2005
  248.8'431--dc22

                                    2005028564

Printed in the United States of America

06 07 08 09 QW 5 4 3 2 1

Beauty does not lie in the face . . .
Beauty is expression. When I paint
a mother I try to render her beautiful
by the mere look she gives her child.

Jean-François Millet

Contents

Introduction 9

1. You have given me beautiful memories to treasure forever 10

2. Your teaching is a light that continually guides me
   through the unknown paths of my life 12

3. You filled my world with beauty and taught me how to appreciate it 14

4. You have done your job well 16

5. You have a special place on your shoulders for catching my tears 18

6. Your passion inspires me to soar high on my own wings 20

7. You taught me that youth and beauty fade, but faith
   blooms more fully in time 24

8. Your heart is like a deep well that keeps on refreshing the
   spirit of your home 26

9. The older you grow, the more beautiful you become 28

10. You show me true forgiveness because you never stop loving me 30

11. You are a woman of character whose strength comes from an
    abiding hope 32

12. Your self-disciplined lifestyle is an inspiration to all who follow you 34

13. Sugar and spice make daughters nice, and it all begins in
    your wonderful kitchen 38

14. Thank you for teaching me through your example how to love others 40

15. When I look in the mirror, I see a reflection of what I've learned from you ... 42

16. Your love of nature's majestic world is a gift you keep giving away 44

17. The best way you've shown your love to me is through listening 46

18. I've never outgrown wanting to share a tea party with you 48

19. Your dreams for me are an unfading hope when life gets tough 52

20. Through watching you persevere through trials, I'm learning to
    do the same 54

21. The strength of your convictions has given me courage to
    stand strong on my own 56

22. Your love is the first love I experienced and truly understood 58

23. You are always there to lift me up 60

24. My joys and sorrows aren't complete until I share them with you, Mom ... 62

25. Thank you for sharing with me the rich heritage of our ancestors 66

26. Our friendship has blossomed over the years through
    your love and patience 68

27. Your actions and lifestyle speak louder than your words 70

28. You know the divine secrets of healing, from kissing bruises to
    soothing wounded hearts 72

29. Your love is like holding a piece of heaven in my heart 74

30. Thank you for being patient as I watch the purpose of my life unfold 76

31. You planted dreams firmly in my heart and watched the
    colorful garden grow 78

32. Your words of encouragement inspire me to keep going
    and to do my best 82

33. You know that a cheerful heart is the best medicine 84

34. You have always kept my life in your praying hands 86

35. Fear has no place in the heart of a daughter who's blessed
    with perfect love 88

36. You never tell my deepest secrets when I share them with you 90

37. Through opening your life to me, I'm drawn to your wellspring of hope   92

38. Thank you for showing me that it's okay to be real instead of perfect 96

39. Your joyful heart creates a home full of love 98

40. Becoming a mother is a journey that begins in childhood 100

41. Thank you for giving me freedom to make my own choices 102

42. Your life leaves footsteps of hope for me to follow 104

43. You always know best how to nourish my mind, body, and soul 106

44. There's little that a mother-daughter shopping spree can't cure 110

45. Through watching you give to others, I've learned to put others first   112

46. Your joyful heart comes from a deep peace within 114

47. You turn the ordinary into the extraordinary 116

48. Your homemade traditions have created a unique source
    of happy memories 118

49. You've shown me that God is the source of all wisdom 120

50. The legacy of your love continues onward to future generations 122

Introduction

There's no one else like you in the world, Mom. The very fact that I'm alive today is because you loved and cared for me from the beginning. Looking back over my years growing up, I see how you poured everything into raising me. Now my heart overflows with gratitude. No matter where I live in this world, I'll always take a part of you with me.

Your faith inspires mine. Your dreams live in my heart. Your hope and joy are part of my soul. I'm a person who's living well all because of you. I'm thankful to be your daughter, and I'll always love you.

The more I live, the more I appreciate your strength and your convictions. I love you, Mom.

> Most of all the other beautiful things in life come by twos or threes, by dozens and hundreds. Plenty of roses, stars, sunsets . . . but only one mother in the whole world.
>
> Kate Douglas Wiggin

Love suffers long and is kind; love does not envy; love does not parade itself, is not puffed up; does not behave rudely, does not seek its own, is not provoked, thinks no evil; does not rejoice in iniquity, but rejoices in the truth.

1 Corinthians 13:4–6 NKJV

You have given me beautiful memories to treasure forever.

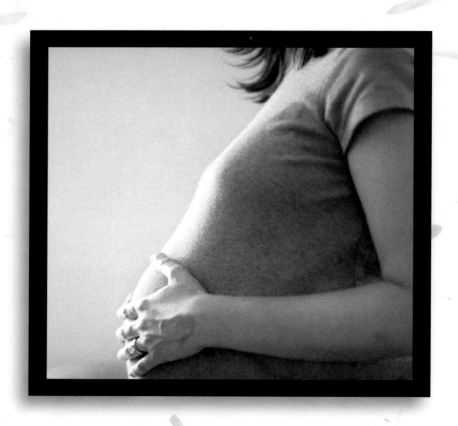

Thank you for taking the time to store all the special seasons of my life in your heart.

I know how special I am to you because you took the time to record my life story. Before I was born, you were waiting for me. You carefully recorded the details of my birth and took pictures of me as an infant. I know how busy you must have been during that time in your life, but those pictures mean so much to me now that I'm older. I know all about my childhood because you told me stories of things I said and things I did while growing up. When I was an adolescent and felt like I couldn't wait to become an adult, you told me what a beautiful person I'd become. These memories wouldn't be there if it weren't for you. Mom, you are loved and treasured.

Oh, better than the minting of a gold-crowned king is the safe-kept memory of a lovely thing.

Sara Teasdale

I thank my God upon every remembrance of you, always
in every prayer of mine making request for you all with joy.

Philippians 1:3–4 NKJV

Your teaching is a light that continually guides me through the unknown paths of my life.

I can't thank you enough for teaching me how to make decisions based on wisdom and truth.

During my younger years, I didn't realize how much you were constantly teaching me and molding my character. Every day, I had to make hundreds of decisions on my own. Sometimes I made mistakes, and you helped me learn to make better choices. When I thought it wasn't a big deal whom I hung out with or dated, you reminded me that I deserved the best. Looking back, I can see that you knew what was good for me, and I know now how much I needed your guidance. Your words of wisdom have been a guide for me all these years. I hope now that you can see some fruit from all that constant teaching. You gave me convictions that keep me pointed toward truth and encourage me to stand strong.

The mother is and must be, whether she knows it or not, the greatest, strongest, and most lasting teacher her children have.

Hannah Whitall Smith

These commands and this teaching are a lamp to light the way ahead of you. The correction of discipline is the way to life.

Proverbs 6:23 NLT

You filled my world with beauty and taught me how to appreciate it.

I learned the art of making a home beautiful through years of watching and learning from you.

You have a passion for beautiful things, and I'm so glad you share this with me. I can see in your eyes and hear in your voice when your creativity is inspired. You can't wait to show me your latest find. When I was younger, you taught me how to arrange a simple bouquet of wildflowers in an elegant crystal vase. You hung my simple drawings and paintings as if they were Monet masterpieces, and you decorated our home with personality and love. I'm amazed at how you can transform a plain dining table into a delightful gathering place for company. I'm trying to do the same. No matter where I live in the future, I'll always look for ways to bring beauty into my world.

A thing of beauty is a joy forever: Its loveliness increases; it can never pass into nothingness.

John Keats

I am the rose of Sharon, and the lily of the valleys.

Song of Solomon 2:1 NKJV

You have done your job well.

Thank you, Mom, for all the sacrifices you made to give me a warm and happy childhood.

Mom, you are so incredibly patient with me. You hung in there with me when I was younger and didn't know enough to show you much gratitude. I took your sacrifices for granted. I kept you busy finding my lost shoes, washing my clothes, and keeping up with my busy schedule. While our family was still asleep, I knew you were up organizing and preparing for the day. In the afternoon, you drove a car full of noisy kids all over town and acted as though it was fun. Somehow you found time to cook dinner, and we all slowed down to share a meal together. During those years I was so absorbed in my own little world that I forgot to thank you. But now I realize how much you did—and still do!—and my heart overflows with grateful love.

Mother taught me by her example of home and hospitality that there's nothing more satisfying than a personal love relationship with the Lord. It's what made her strong.

Anne Graham Lotz

Many women have done excellently, but you surpass them all.

Proverbs 31:29 NRSV

You have a special place on your shoulders for catching my tears.

Thank you for teaching me how to recover from discouragement and move on with hope for the future.

I remember so many times when I held in my tears until I reached your arms. There were days when my friends said mean things to me or made me feel left out. I hid those painful feelings of rejection until I got to you. I never had to worry that you'd laugh at my problems or think they were silly. You listened to me and soothed my wounds with gentle words. When I was a little girl, sometimes all it took was a hug. But in more recent years when my heart was crushed, I didn't know if I'd ever make it through those disappointments. But you always said to me, "I think you're wonderful." You caught my tears of pain and helped me grow stronger from them.

Who ran to help me when I fell, and would some pretty story tell, or kiss the place to make it well? My mother.

Ann Taylor

Those who sow in tears will reap with songs of joy.

Psalm 126:5 NIV

Your passion inspires me to soar high on my own wings.

Thank you for leading me to the One who will never let me go.

When I was a baby, you held me physically close to your heart. You wrapped me in a soft pink blanket and sang gentle lullabies to me. Then you let go a bit when I began to notice the world around me. You watched and taught as I began to crawl, then toddle, and eventually run. You were preparing me to become independent. I understand now that sometimes the process of letting go can be painful. Your knees ached from hours of prayer. Your deepest desire was to see me develop wisdom based on eternal truths, and you continued to love and inspire me in this direction. Although you can't hold my hand forever, your guidance has led me to the One who can.

Children are not so different from kites. Children were created to fly. But they need wind, the undergirding and strength that come from unconditional love, encouragement, and prayer.

Gigi Graham

The LORD says, "I will guide you along the best pathway for your life. I will advise you and watch over you."

Psalm 32:8 NLT

Mom, you are loved and treasured.

You gave me convictions that
keep me pointed toward truth
and encourage me to stand strong.

I realize how much you do, and my
heart overflows with grateful love.

You taught me that youth and beauty fade, but faith blooms more fully in time.

You taught me about real beauty and helped me become a person of faith.

It's so easy for a girl to get caught up in focusing on her outer looks. Every magazine cover displays the newest beauty secrets, quick ways to lose weight, and styling tips of the stars. I always longed for acceptance, and I used to think that trendy outfits and my appearance would make me popular. Yet you told me something different. You reminded me that it isn't outer beauty that really matters; it's what's inside. Your words helped my faith ripen day by day, and I realized how very special you are. You taught me to look beyond fashion trends to search for that hidden treasure of faith. In doing so, I became aware of my real beauty and learned where to find a peace beyond what the world has to offer.

> Beauty from the heart is what brings glory to God.
>
> Heather Whitestone McCallum

Your beauty should consist of your true inner self,
the ageless beauty of a gentle and quiet spirit,
which is of the greatest value in God's sight.

1 Peter 3:4 GNT

Your heart is like a deep well that keeps on refreshing the spirit of your home.

Your gift of encouraging others with your words makes your home a friendly place of fellowship.

In The Wizard of Oz, Dorothy said it best when she clicked her red shoes together three times, reciting, "There's no place like home." It's true. I always felt our home was the one place where I could kick off my shoes and be myself. The main reason is that you worked hard to make sure our home had a positive atmosphere of love. Your words of encouragement refreshed everyone who walked in the door. Even on days when I came home cranky and tired, you knew how to lift me back up again. I enjoyed bringing home company because you said the nicest things to my friends. You know how to bring out the best in people, and everyone feels welcome in your home.

Praise will transform the humblest dwelling to a hallowed heaven.

Frances J. Roberts

The generous prosper and are satisfied; those who refresh others will themselves be refreshed.

Proverbs 11:25 NLT

The older you grow, the more beautiful you become.

Your years of life experience have polished you so that you sparkle like a rare and precious jewel.

You have become more radiant with beauty as the years have gone by. You are a precious gem, sparkling in brilliance. You've been chipped, refined, and polished so that your jewel-like qualities are no longer hidden. The process of growing older has deepened your faith, and I love hearing about what's made you more beautiful with each passing year. Since your schedule's slowed down a bit, you have more time to sit and chat with me. As you share the refining processes you've been through, I'm discovering how to focus on the truly meaningful things in life. I'm still rough around the edges, but my greatest hope is that one day my faith will shimmer like yours and that I, too, will radiate a deep, timeless beauty.

Beauty does not lie in the face . . . Beauty is expression. When I paint a mother I try to render her beautiful by the mere look she gives her child.

Jean-François Millet

We set our eyes not on what we see but on what we cannot see. What we see will last only a short time, but what we cannot see will last forever.

2 Corinthians 4:18 NCV

You show me true forgiveness because you never stop loving me.

Even when I'm at fault, your love overwhelms me with true forgiveness.

I'm sorry. Those two words have always been so hard for me to say, even when I knew some of my angry words really hurt your feelings. Yet you have always forgiven me. Time is precious, and you didn't want to waste days or months harboring a grudge. I watched other mother-daughter relationships suffer from pain and heartache, but you never let go of me. Your forgiveness goes beyond comprehension. I learned from you how I need to forgive others who say hurtful things to me as well. Despite my shortcomings, you continually show me that the power of love can bind even the most wounded of hearts. Because of you, I learned to appreciate the overwhelming compassion God has for us. It's also against His nature to ever stop loving.

> The heart of a mother is a deep abyss at the bottom of which you will always find forgiveness.
>
> Honoré de Balzac

Be kind to one another, tenderhearted, forgiving one another, just as God in Christ forgave you.

Ephesians 4:32 NKJV

You are a woman of character whose strength comes from an abiding hope.

I want to be more like you in choosing to have hope that tomorrow is a new and brighter day.

If I could describe you in one word, I'd say you're *optimistic*. You always look on the bright side of things and choose to let go of the negative. I wish I could be more like you in that way. Your glass is never half empty; it's half full, and you look around to find someone to share it with. Things haven't always gone right in your life, but you chose to remain hopeful that tomorrow is a new and better day. People are drawn to you because you don't let anything get you down. I didn't always know that hope is a choice. I thought either you had it or you didn't. Now I see that you chose to let hope be the anchor of your soul.

> Hope is like the sun, which, as we journey toward it, casts the shadow of our burden behind us.
>
> Samuel Smiles

The LORD is good to those whose hope is in him, to the one who seeks him; it is good to wait quietly for the salvation of the LORD.

Lamentations 3:25–26 NIV

Your self-disciplined lifestyle is an inspiration to all who follow you.

I learned from you how to make the best use of the precious time I am given.

A single day is made up of 1,440 minutes. No more, no less. Some people fritter away the precious time they are given, but you aren't one of them. Everyone who knows you is inspired by the dreams you reach, the goals you accomplish, and the lifestyle you live. It is no surprise that you are also a model of self-discipline and that you gave me a vision for my own life. You tell me to fill my mind with pure, positive thoughts and to not dwell on the negative. The friends you spend time with are also women who lead you onward and upward instead of dragging you down. Your self-controlled habits have become ingrained in me, and I'm inspired to make the best use of every moment.

Make each day useful and cheerful . . . by employing it well. Then youth will be happy, old age without regret, and life a beautiful success.

Louisa May Alcott

You yourself must be an example to them by doing good deeds of every kind. Let everything you do reflect the integrity and seriousness of your teaching.

Titus 2:7 NLT

You chose to let hope be the
anchor of your soul.

You continually show me that the
power of love can bind even the
most wounded of hearts.

Because of you, I learned to appreciate the
overwhelming compassion God has for us.

Sugar and spice make daughters nice, and it all begins in your wonderful kitchen.

I'm thankful you took the time to teach me how to prepare meals and be hospitable.

The whirring sound of a mixer always brings back pleasant memories of my learning to cook at your side. Even when the eggs didn't quite crack into the bowl, you still let me be your helper. I remember the sweet smell of cake in the oven as we prepared for someone's special event. You let me pick out the candles and help decorate with colored icing. During the holidays, you taught me how to make special gifts to surprise my teachers and others. You knew that by showing me how to cook, I'd someday have the skills to refresh those around me with hospitality. You rescued me many times by teaching me how to salvage a culinary disaster. I'm still learning and using everything you taught me.

A mother is a person who, seeing there are only four pieces of pie for five people, promptly announces she never did care for pie.

Tenneva Jordan

When God's children are in need, be the one to help them out. And get into the habit of inviting guests home for dinner or, if they need lodging, for the night.

Romans 12:13 NLT

Thank you for teaching me through your example how to love others.

I learned from you that love has two hands that serve others cheerfully.

Love is not just a word to you; it's an action. I've watched you love others through serving and giving, even when you knew they could never return the favor. During the holiday season, we dropped coins in the bell ringer's bucket and wished that cheerful servant a merry Christmas. You let me come along with you to deliver meals to those who needed help, and I saw what a difference it made. When I started envying all the things my friends had that I wanted, you took me to a different part of town where I saw people struggling to get by. I made a habit of going through my toys and clothes to see what I could share. Your lifestyle of giving your best to others has become deeply ingrained in my character.

A mother's love is like a circle; it has no beginning and no ending. It keeps going around and around ever expanding, touching everyone who comes in contact with it.

Art Urban

Love one another earnestly with all your heart.

1 Peter 1:22 GNT

When I look in the mirror, I see a reflection of what I've learned from you.

I'm proud to go through life as a reflection of you and all you've taught me.

I love hearing someone say to me, "You remind me so much of your mother." It wasn't always this way. I went through a phase where I rolled my eyes behind your back and felt like you were so far from understanding the *real* me. I'm embarrassed by those actions. But you never gave up on loving me. Now, I'm thankful to look and act like you. Everything I've heard you say over the years is logged away in my memory. I was shocked the first time I realized that I had become a replica of you. Then slowly a feeling of acceptance began to warm my heart. When I look in the mirror, I'm so glad to see your face reflected in mine.

As any daughter can attest, it's eerie when you wake up and realize you're becoming your mother. Thankfully for me, that's a good thing.

Lisa Whelchel

Everyone who likes to use proverbs will use this one:
"Like mother, like daughter."

Ezekiel 16:44 MSG

*Your love of nature's majestic world
is a gift you keep giving away.*

*When you taught me to notice the world
around me, you taught me to appreciate
the divine beauty of nature.*

Whenever a new season begins, I always think of you. The purple crocus and yellow jonquil blooms remind me of your zeal for colorful gardens. As spring gives way to summer, I think back to beach trips where we built sand castles to the sound of the rolling surf. In autumn, when leaves turn red and gold, I remember our taking walks and picking up pretty leaves to press in a book. Next, you welcomed the frost of winter by telling us maybe we'd wake up to a white-powdered dusting of snow. I'm so glad you took time to answer my questions about nature, instilling in me a sense of awe about the great outdoors. Most of all, you made sure I knew who created this ever-changing display of the seasons.

The kiss of sun for pardon, the song of birds for mirth—one is nearer God's heart in a garden than anywhere else on earth.

Dorothy Gurney

By the word of the LORD were the heavens made, their starry host by the breath of his mouth.

Psalm 33:6 NIV

*The best way you've shown your
love to me is through listening.*

*Thanks for letting me open up and express
my deepest thoughts with you.*

Women love to talk. It's been said that, on average, we say more than four thousand words per day. I can't deny that's true. But it's no fun to talk if there's not a good listener around, and you're the best. I don't have to break the ice or hide my true feelings when I talk to you. I never have to worry about saying the wrong thing or sounding ridiculous. You know how to listen without interrupting, even when I'm telling you about my terrible, horrible, bad-hair, stuck-in-the mud day. No one else in the world would care, but you make me feel like I'm the most interesting person in the world. You take everything in, making me feel like life is good.

A mother is she who can take the place of all others but whose place no one else can take.

Gaspard Mermillod

Be quick to listen, slow to speak, and slow to get angry.

James 1:19 NLT

I've never outgrown wanting to share a tea party with you.

Our grown-up tea parties give a sweet aroma to the rich bonds of our lifetime friendship.

I remember how much I enjoyed having tea parties when I was a little girl. Sometimes it was just me and my dolls, but often you were the honored guest. You showed me how to place a napkin in my lap and act like a lady. "Would you care for a cup of tea?" I asked as I poured water from a pink plastic teapot. We laughed then, as we still do now. Though many years have passed, there's nothing I enjoy more than sharing a hot cup of tea or coffee with you. We don't need anything fancy, just some caffeine to perk us up. Whether we make a special trip to a tea shop or we hold steaming mugs at the kitchen table, our times together leave me feeling so refreshed.

Line by line, moment by moment, special times are etched into our memories in the permanent ink of everlasting love in our relationships.

Gloria Gaither

The memory of the righteous will be a blessing.

Proverbs 10:7 NIV

Love is not just a word to you;
it's an action.

You make me feel like I'm the most
interesting person in the world.

When I look in the mirror, I'm so glad
to see your face reflected in mine.

Your dreams for me are an unfading hope when life gets tough.

A daughter learns to aim high in life to fulfill the dreams her mother placed in her heart.

When I was growing up, I always felt like a royal princess in your eyes. You made me believe I was poised, intelligent, and captivating. You told me I could sing with the voice of an angel and dance with the grace of a prima ballerina. I thought I was a genius from the way you praised my accomplishments to others. When I started school, I thought everyone would think this same way about me. But of course that wasn't true. Even when I did my best, there was usually someone else way ahead of me. At times I got discouraged and didn't know if I'd ever amount to anything. But you kept telling me to aim high with my dreams. I've always kept your words close within my heart. I've learned to aim high in life to fulfill the dreams you placed in my heart.

> Youth fades; love droops, the leaves of friendship fall; a mother's secret hope outlives them all.
>
> Oliver Wendell Holmes

Remember that I commanded you to be strong and brave. Don't be afraid, because the LORD your God will be with you everywhere you go.

Joshua 1:9 NCV

Through watching you persevere through trials, I'm learning to do the same.

My faith is renewed through seeing you stand strong through difficulty and pain.

A stained-glass window appears dark and plain unless there's light shining through it. Then colors are amplified, radiant with beauty. Like this window, I've watched you become a vibrant work of art as the fire of trials has illuminated your strength. Everyone is amazed at your ability to withstand difficulties that seem impossible. Someone weaker would have faltered when hearing frightening news from the doctor or realizing looming financial distress. But you took it all in stride, turning every disappointment into a prayer of faith. You never give up, and you show me that hope comes from trusting God with every situation, good and bad. Because of you, I'm learning where to turn when trials come my way as well.

> The strengthening of faith comes through staying with it in the hour of trial.
>
> Catherine Marshall

We also boast in our sufferings, knowing that suffering produces endurance, and endurance produces character, and character produces hope.

Romans 5:3–4 NRSV

The strength of your convictions has given me courage to stand strong on my own.

I'm thankful that you taught me to base my convictions on truth that never changes.

Every day I'm bombarded with voices trying to sway me to believe one idea or another. I hear one point of view on the radio, and then I read a completely different opinion in a book. I hang out with different types of people, and some believe one thing and some another. I'm so glad I don't have to be confused about my value system. I know I can constantly return to the convictions you taught me that are based on God's truth. When I hear something that doesn't measure up against the straightedge of the Bible, I can let it go. You told me over and over that if I don't stand strong for something, I'll fall for anything. I feel like my courage is rooted in your strength.

> Keep your fears to yourself, but share your courage with others.
>
> Robert Louis Stevenson

If you do not stand firm in your faith, you will not stand at all.

Isaiah 7:9 NIV

Your love is the first love I experienced and truly understood.

Thanks for teaching me about the kind of love that never ends, from one generation to the next.

The bond of love between us is permanent, and I know nothing will ever change the way you feel about me. I'm fascinated by this deep relationship between a mother and her daughter. The thread of devotion between us mirrors centuries of unconditional love between girls and their moms. Your love echoes that of God's love for His children: perfect and unchanging. As I've matured, I've discovered the heartache that sometimes comes with romantic love; it can be thriving one day and gone the next. But no matter what I say or do, I know you'll never stop loving me. I have complete freedom to be myself. You have given me the ability to love others beyond my own strength. The cycle never ends.

In the sheltered simplicity of the first days after a baby's born, one sees again the magical closed circle, the miraculous sense of two people existing only for each other.

Anne Morrow Lindbergh

He tends his flock like a shepherd: he gathers the lambs
in his arms and carries them close to his heart;
he gently leads those that have young.

Isaiah 40:11 NIV

You are always there to lift me up.

*Thanks, Mom, for always being available
to help carry my sometimes heavy load.*

I've been through times when I've felt completely worn out and defeated, with not even an ounce of energy left. Every fiber in me wanted to scream, "I give up!" Day after day, I've felt those waves of pressure come crashing on top of me. I've worried about relationships, my future, and my finances to no end. Those times when I've reached the end of my rope, I've called you in desperation. Just a few minutes of talking to you has changed everything. You've said to me so many times, "This, too, shall pass." As I share my stresses and fears with you, you take part of the burden on yourself. I know you'll pray for me and help me find peace.

True mothers have to be made of steel to withstand the difficulties that are sure to beset their children.

Rachel Billington

Come to me, all you that are weary and are carrying heavy burdens, and I will give you rest.

Matthew 11:28 NRSV

My joys and sorrows aren't complete until I share them with you, Mom.

I love being able to share the happy and sad events of my life with someone who cares so much.

When something wonderful happens in my life, you are the first person I want to share it with. You are never jealous of my success; you make me feel that you're so proud of me. I love watching your face light up when I've had a great experience. Since part of you lives inside me, we go through all these big events together. Then there are the not-so-happy things I can't wait to tell you. You weep with me as I come to you time and again with my feelings of rejection and brokenness. I just don't feel as if my emotions are complete until I share them with you. When I do, my joys are instantly doubled and my sorrows are split in half, and usually thrown right out the window.

All who would win joy must share it. Happiness was born a twin.

Lord Byron

Rejoice with those who rejoice, and weep with those who weep.

Romans 12:15 NKJV

You told me over and over that if
I don't stand strong for something,
I'll fall for anything.

Because of you, I'm learning where to
turn when trials come my way.

I've learned to aim high in life to fulfill
the dreams you placed in my heart.

Thank you for sharing with me the
rich heritage of our ancestors.

I feel strong because you took the
time to teach me about my roots.

I've never had to wonder about who my family is. You've made sure I know all about my wonderful, rich heritage. I love hearing stories about you when you were a little girl, and I can see myself in your personality when you were my age. You've worked hard over the years to make sure I spend plenty of time with relatives who don't live near me. Now that some of them have passed on, I cherish these memories all the more. Knowing my roots makes me stronger, like a tree that is planted deep into fertile soil. I'm not going to blow over in a storm, because I know our ancestors struggled and survived through much harder times.

The proper time to influence the character of a child is about a hundred years before he is born.

Dean Inge

A good name is to be chosen rather than great riches,
loving favor rather than silver and gold.

Proverbs 22:1 NKJV

Our friendship has blossomed over the years through your love and patience.

You are my best friend, and I'm looking forward to creating new memories with you in the future.

It's been a gradual process, but I'm amazed at how close we've become. The generation gap has narrowed between us. Because you always listened to me, you know more about me than anyone else in the world. You cultivated our relationship with patience, showering it with love and forgiveness. I know I needed some stubborn weeds pulled as I grew up, but you nurtured me with the best of care. If everyone else deserts me, I know I have you—my mother, my friend. You are all I need. I'm so thankful for the intimacy we're able to share. Just as there is no other fragrance as sweet and pure as a rose, there is no other friendship as beautiful as that between a mom and her little girl.

A mother is the truest friend we have, when trials, heavy and sudden, fall upon us . . . still will she cling to us . . . and cause peace to return to our hearts.

Washington Irving

A friend loves at all times.

Proverbs 17:17 NIV

*Your actions and lifestyle speak
louder than your words.*

*I'm following your example in
making the choices that will lead
to a richly fulfilling life.*

Through the years, I've learned that many people say they believe one thing, but the reality of their lives doesn't show it. It has never been that way with you. Your lifestyle made a deep imprint on my heart. I've watched you make decisions, some big, some small. Those choices have had more of an impact on me than anything you could ever say to me. Instead of focusing on your own needs, you find ways to help others. When someone hurts your feelings, you choose to forgive immediately instead of holding a grudge. You think positive thoughts and take delight in the pure joy of living, even during tough times. Mom, I want to be a woman who lives like you, because I know I'll have a lifestyle with no regrets.

> God isn't as concerned with how boldly you speak for him as he is with how boldly you live for him.
>
> Martha Bolton

Someone will say, "One person has faith, another has actions."
My answer is, "Show me how anyone can have faith without actions.
I will show you my faith by my actions."

James 2:18 GNT

*You know the divine secrets of
healing, from kissing bruises
to soothing wounded hearts.*

*Your healing words show me that
every dark cloud is lined with a
glimmering trace of silver.*

I don't always want to ask for help when I'm discouraged, but I'm so thankful you're there. More than once, you've helped me pick up the pieces of a broken dream. You never rub salt in my wounds, but instead gently apply healing salve where I hurt most. If you can't think of the right thing to say, you lead me to the words I need to hear through an uplifting book or a friend. In time I understand whether I'm to glue the pieces of my dream back together or move on to create something new. You taught me that the secret to healing is turning to God, the source of our comfort. If I can seek Him during my stressful times, His Word refreshes me and renews my hope.

You will have as much joy and laughter in life as faith in God.

Martin Luther

He heals the brokenhearted, and binds up their wounds.

Psalm 147:3 NRSV

Your love is like holding a piece of heaven in my heart.

I feel accepted for who I am because of the way you love me unconditionally.

Everywhere I turn, I hear about step-by-step action plans and programs that promise to change my life if I stick with them. *Five quick tips to save money, six strategies for losing weight, eight ways to get what I want from people.* I'm so glad there are no secret strategies for working my way into your heart or earning your admiration. I don't have to do anything to receive your love. You love me for who I am, even if I'm far from perfect. I may fall short of accomplishment in the eyes of program developers, but I never fail in your eyes. Your love mirrors God's everlasting love for His children. I've learned so much about God's deep, eternal love through the way you cherish me.

With the obvious exception of my heavenly Father, my mother has had the greatest influence on me, from the inside out.

Lisa Whelchel

Let love and faithfulness never leave you . . .
write them on the tablet of your heart.

Proverbs 3:3 NIV

Thank you for being patient as I watch
the purpose of my life unfold.

I've discovered that one of my life goals
is to become a mom just like you.

When I was a little girl, I remember everybody asking me what I wanted to be when I grew up. Although I changed my mind with every new interest, you thought that was fine. You allowed me to learn about my strengths and weaknesses through personal experience. Slowly I began to discover what passions made my heart beat a little faster. As I embarked on this journey of purpose, sometimes the path was clear to me and other times I walk only in faith. Your inspiration and patience helped me feel room to explore. When I reached a dead end, I knew to look for a different route. As it turns out, I'm moving steadily toward becoming a woman like you, who encourages others to follow their dreams as well.

Either we are adrift in chaos or we are individuals, created, loved, upheld and placed purposefully, exactly where we are. Can you believe that? Can you trust God for that?

Elisabeth Elliot

I know the thoughts that I think toward you, says the LORD, thoughts of peace and not of evil, to give you a future and a hope.

Jeremiah 29:11 NKJV

*You planted dreams firmly in my heart
and watched the colorful garden grow.*

*All my gifts have been cultivated by your
years of encouragement and prayer.*

I can't thank you enough for sowing tiny seeds within me that have bloomed over the years. You helped me uncover my gifts. As I tried out new interests, I know you were praying that I'd find something I really enjoyed doing. I remember times when I excelled in an activity, as well as times when I performed miserably. But you kept motivating me to stick out the season and try my best. Your dreams for me went beyond the tangible; you wanted me to become a well-balanced adult with something to offer others. Now, I see how all those experiences have fueled my life goals. I may not be an Olympic medalist or a performer at Carnegie Hall, but I've learned to cultivate the unique talents within me.

The days may come, the days may go; but still the hands of memories weave the blissful dreams of long ago.

George Cooper

I am sure that God, who began this good work in you, will carry it on until it is finished on the Day of Christ Jesus.

Philippians 1:6 GNT

Just as there is no other fragrance as sweet and pure as a rose, there is no other friendship as beautiful as that between a mom and her little girl.

I've never had to wonder about who my family is. You've made sure I know all about my wonderful, rich heritage.

Mom, I want to be a woman who lives like you, because I know I'll have a lifestyle with no regrets.

Your words of encouragement inspire me to keep going and to do my best.

Thank you for encouraging me to stay focused on what really matters and to not let distractions pull me down.

I love watching dancers twirl in graceful circles. It seems they can spin forever without getting dizzy. I know it's because they've been trained to concentrate on a focal point. Dancers maintain their defined movements and poise because they're not distracted. I wish I could do the same. Sometimes I feel like I'm spinning aimlessly in sixteen directions, but you taught me how to focus. It's a blessing to hear your voice motivating me to keep my heart in the right place. Your encouraging words build up my character and remind me to center on truth. When I listen to you, distractions in my life fall away. Like a dancer with a focal point, I can move through my days with strength and grace.

Those who bring sunshine to the lives of others cannot keep it from themselves.

James M. Barrie

Pleasant words are a honeycomb,
sweet to the soul and healing to the bones.

Proverbs 16:24 NIV

*You know that a cheerful
heart is the best medicine.*

*Your gift of laughter spreads a joy that's
contagious to me and everyone around you.*

Laughter is a gift that you share with me over and over. You find the humor in so many of life's crazy moments. I now see that it's a deliberate way of thinking. This attitude of cheer comes from keeping a godly perspective on what really matters. It's fun now to look back over our cache of memories and find humor in our life events. The day that seemed so awful now seems hilarious. The tears of sadness have now turned into tears of joy. You helped me let go of pain and replace pain with hope. Your heart contains joy that you share with others, and laughter is a tangible way to love. What a precious gift you gave me.

Laughter dulls the sharpest pain and flattens out the greatest stress. To share it is to give a gift of health.

Barbara Johnson

A cheerful look brings joy to the heart; good news makes for good health.

Proverbs 15:30 NLT

*You have always kept my
life in your praying hands.*

*Your prayers ensured that I
never had to face the world
without God's guidance and love.*

What was it like for you the first time I went somewhere alone? It must have been hard to let me go out into the world. You couldn't control what my eyes, heart, and mind were exposed to. I know that you prayed I would be drawn to purity instead of being enticed by evil. There were probably times you worried about me. You didn't know who or what was influencing my heart. Over the years, I've struggled and grown in my convictions. You never forced me to take on your faith; you just demonstrated a steadfast sense of peace that God would lead me to Himself. I know your prayers have saved me from many dangers, and in return, I can now pray for you with the same deep faith.

I have held many things in my hands, and I have lost them all; but whatever I have placed in God's hands, that I still possess.

Corrie ten Boom

The prayer of the righteous is powerful and effective.

James 5:16 NRSV

Fear has no place in the heart of a daughter who's blessed with perfect love.

Thanks, Mom, for helping me replace my worries and fears with trust that God will take care of me.

As I'm learning to navigate my way through life, I sometimes feel afraid. I don't know what's around the next corner, and I'm not sure if I'm doing the right thing. I can lose sleep wondering about the *what-ifs* and the *if-onlys*. It's hard to admit that I often let fear and worry choke out my joy. You always remind me to find tiny things to be thankful for every day. In turning my worries into prayers, I can feel God's peace flowing through me. You taught me to look for ways to help others instead of turning inward and being consumed by my self-centered fears. Most of all, you pointed me to Scripture, which fuels me with perfect love and helps me find purpose in all I do.

> The mother love is like God's love; he loves us not because we are lovable, but because it is his nature to love, and because we are his children.
>
> Earl Riney

There is no fear in love; but perfect love casts out fear.

1 John 4:18 NKJV

You never tell my deepest secrets when I share them with you.

You're the one person in the world I can trust with all my most private thoughts and feelings.

I'm so thankful I can trust you with my deepest feelings. You work your way gently into my heart and help me figure out how I really feel. I can share my experiences with you in confidence that you won't tell others without my permission. I know there are some people in the world I can't trust with a secret thought. If I told them my innermost feelings, they'd go and spill my secrets to someone else. But I need someone to share with, and it means a lot to me to have you. Even when I'm way off in my thinking, you steer me in the right direction without telling others about my zany ideas. It's pure refreshment to be able to tell you everything on my heart.

> The child rejoices in the mother; not in her promises, but in herself.
>
> Hannah Whitall Smith

No one who gossips can be trusted with a secret,
but you can put confidence in someone who is trustworthy.

Proverbs 11:13 GNT

Through opening your life to me, I'm drawn to your wellspring of hope.

I feel blessed that you've let me enter the depths of your heart, where your faith lies open and true.

I never have to wonder about what's taking place in your heart. You are always open with me. You aren't afraid to share with me what you're thinking about. Your memories of the past and dreams for the future are part of my life as well. I appreciate your openness, as you admit your struggles at times. I'm drawn to your deep inner core of courage and hope that I know lies beneath the surface. It makes me feel close to you when you allow me to share in your passions and faith. You always say that any good that comes from you is a result of God's work in you. You fill me with the inspiration that someday I'll have something to share with others that will bring them hope as well.

If we faithfully nurture what is beneath the surface of our life, people will marvel at what they see of God in us!

Elizabeth George

I pray that the God who gives hope will fill you with much joy and peace . . . Then your hope will overflow by the power of the Holy Spirit.

Romans 15:13 NCV

Your encouraging words build
up my character and remind
me to center on truth.

You never forced me to take on
your faith; you just demonstrated
a steadfast sense of peace that
God would lead me to Himself.

You pointed me to Scripture,
which fuels me with perfect love
and helps me find purpose in all I do.

Thank you for showing me that it's
okay to be real instead of perfect.

I can relax around you because
you surround me with the grace
of unconditional love.

When I look back at old photos, I laugh when I see a silly, fake smile across my face. Even though I may have grinned for the camera, my eyes reveal how I really felt about having my picture made. Yet I often do the same thing now. I tell people, "I'm fine. Everything's perfect!" when actually I'm just afraid they won't like the real me. But with you, it's okay to be myself. I love the feeling of relaxation I get when I'm around you. It comes from your unconditional love and acceptance of who I am. You'd rather I tell the truth than hide behind a shallow image of perfection. I want to extend this love to others and not judge them superficially. It's called grace.

Believing that you are loved will set you free to be who God created you to be. So rest in His love and just be yourself.

Lisa Whelchel

My grace is sufficient for you, for my power is made perfect in weakness.

2 Corinthians 12:9 NIV

*Your joyful heart creates
a home full of love.*

*I've learned from you that
an atmosphere of joy is created
and sustained by a mother.*

The fragrance of joy lingers throughout your house. I know as soon as I walk in the door that I can leave my tension and worries at the doorstep. You always set a tone of peace inside your home. Whereas I tend to let my moods be dictated by circumstances, you have a joy that transcends what's happening in your life. It has only been in recent years that I have realized how hard it must be for you to maintain continual joy. You must have exhausting days, but they don't turn you into a bitter complainer. I'm determined to let my joy come from my faith instead of my circumstances as well. Just as yours does, I want the attitude of my heart to create a haven of peace.

Our home joys are the most delightful earth affords, and the joy of parents in their children is the most holy joy of humanity.

Johann Heinrich Pestalozzi

Let the hearts of those rejoice who seek the LORD!
Seek the LORD and His strength; seek His face evermore!

1 Chronicles 16:10–11 NKJV

Becoming a mother is a journey that begins in childhood.

You showed me that mothering is an art, achieved only through years of faithful practice.

I didn't realize it as I was growing up, but you were constantly teaching me about motherhood. You took my natural instincts to nurture and to love, and you gave me plenty of practice. You didn't laugh at me when I felt motherly toward my ladybug collection or midnight jar of twinkling fireflies. You let me learn about responsibility by giving me other pets to take care of. I discovered through your teaching that all living things need steadfast love, care, and attention. As soon as I was old enough, you guided me toward jobs that involved tending the needs of others. You knew those experiences would help me someday. My journey continues. I'm realizing now how much goes into becoming a mom, and I appreciate you all the more.

We never know the love of the parent till we become parents ourselves.

Henry Ward Beecher

To everything there is a season,
a time for every purpose under heaven.

Ecclesiastes 3:1 NKJV

*Thank you for giving me freedom
to make my own choices.*

*I've become an independent
thinker because you allowed me
freedom to learn on my own.*

I know there were probably times when you wished I could be trained like a robot to follow your commands. *Do this. Don't do that. Think this. Don't think that.* My life would have been much easier if I'd followed your advice and example right away. But you gave me the freedom to voice my opinions and make my own decisions. It must have hurt you at times to see me make mistakes. Yet you knew that personal experience is often the best and only teacher. Within your guidelines and boundaries, I felt free to think and act independently. Now I see how learning by trial and error strengthened my leadership abilities. I don't have to follow the crowd. Instead, I make my own choices based on what I believe is right.

> As a mother, my job is to take care of what is impossible and trust God with the possible.
>
> Ruth Bell Graham

I will walk about in freedom, for I have sought out your precepts.

Psalm 119:45 NIV

*Your life leaves footsteps
of hope for me to follow.*

*I'm not afraid to walk an uncertain
path because you already cleared
a trail with your courage.*

Though you don't walk around in hiking boots every day, you are a terrific trailblazer. You aren't concerned with doing the same thing as everyone else. You set high goals and reach for them, leaving a new path for others to follow. I admire your confidence, which I know comes from your belief that God is leading the way. You are not afraid of change, even when it's not exactly what you'd been planning. Instead, you say that each new season of life is the best you ever experienced. You don't long for the past; you march onward toward the future. Your thousand-mile journey is composed of step-by-step courage, and I'm following you. In showing me how to move away from the pack and blaze my own trail, you give me your legacy of hope.

There are only two lasting bequests we can hope to give to our children. One of these is roots; the other is wings.

Hodding Carter

One generation shall praise Your works to another,
and shall declare Your mighty acts.

Psalm 145:4 NKJV

You always know best how to nourish my mind, body, and soul.

I'm thankful to be whole, lacking nothing.

One of your greatest gifts to me is how you brought me up to live a well-balanced life. I'm physically alive, so you made sure I filled my body with nutritious meals. Fresh air and exercise were part of my daily routine, helping me develop lifelong healthy habits. You stimulated my mind by surrounding me with your love of books, music, and interesting people. My emotional needs were met first with your love and protection; then you guided me in establishing relationships that were also good for me. Most important, you delighted in nourishing my soul, in helping me develop my own spiritual walk and faith. The person I've become is a reflection of the steady diet of nourishment you gave me over the years.

Just as the body grows and flourishes on a healthy diet, our joy can grow and flourish when fed a steady diet of beauty.

Thomas Kinkade

Think about the things that are good and worthy of praise. Think about the things that are true and honorable and right and pure and beautiful and respected.

Philippians 4:8 NCV

You took my natural instincts to
nurture and to love, and you
gave me plenty of practice.

I love the feeling of relaxation I get
when I'm around you. It comes
from your unconditional love
and acceptance of who I am.

Just as yours does, I want the attitude of
my heart to create a haven of peace.

There's little that a mother-daughter shopping spree can't cure.

I love bonding with you at the mall as we share compliments and coupons.

I love having an excuse to go shopping with you. The stores may entice us with glamorous advertising, but what really draws us in is the experience of being together. You are the one person who always makes me feel great about myself. "Oh, that color looks wonderful with your eyes!" you'll say to me. Or, "Just think how much you're saving on that outfit with your coupons!" A few words from you make me feel like a princess. When I choose gifts for other people, you compliment me on my good taste and assure me the recipients will *love* what I picked out. As we leave the stores carrying our shopping bags, my heart is full, and our fun memories stay with me a long, long time.

As my girls get older, I realize how blessed I am to have their friendship. They are my best shopping buddies!

Michelle Medlock Adams

Yes, we should make the most of what God gives, both the bounty and the capacity to enjoy it, accepting what's given and delighting in the work. It's God's gift!

Ecclesiastes 5:19 MSG

*Through watching you give to others,
I've learned to put others first.*

*I want my life to be an act of
service to others, like yours.*

When Pastor John Wesley said, "Do all the good you can, by all the means you can, in all the ways you can . . . as long as ever you can," he could have been describing you. Your whole life is an act of service to others. You made sure your family's every need was met, even if it meant making sacrifices. When I think of all the menus you planned, the thousands of hours you grocery-shopped, and the years you hosted company in our home, I'm amazed. You gave me the gift of your undivided attention, even when your favorite TV show was on. You basically put your dreams on hold so that I could realize mine. Your love for others keeps overflowing through a faith that blesses through action.

> Love is an attribute of God. To love others is evidence of a genuine faith.
>
> Kay Arthur

Whenever we have the opportunity, we should do good to everyone, especially to our Christian brothers and sisters.

Galatians 6:10 NLT

*Your joyful heart comes from
a deep peace within.*

*I want my faith to become fully
matured and bear fruit like yours.*

Farmers know that fruit tastes best when it is allowed to ripen naturally in the warm sun. If it is plucked off prematurely, it won't have the same rich flavor. The gifts of rain and sunshine transform tiny spring blossoms into mature, succulent fruit. In my spiritual life, I long to bear fruit as well. Yet joy and peace often elude me in my quick-paced attempt to be more like Christ. You are an example of someone who cultivated the fruits of joy and peace in her life. You work on maturing slowly and gracefully during times of abundance so that when a crisis comes you're prepared to handle it. You are able to maintain an attitude of joy even when a storm threatens to overpower you. That's the kind of spiritual fruit I seek.

Joy is not gush; joy is not mere jolliness. Joy is perfect acquiescence, acceptance, and rest in God's will, whatever comes.

Amy Carmichael

Let the peace of God rule in your hearts, to which also you were called in one body; and be thankful.

Colossians 3:15 NKJV

You turn the ordinary into the extraordinary.

Thank you for showing me how to take delight in the beauty of simplicity.

It takes a mother's touch to see the maximum potential in everything. Your creativity has transformed many a plain day into something special. You taught me to be thankful for rainy afternoons, because that meant special trips to the library or museum. Simple picnic lunches became exciting adventures when you stretched my imagination to play games and fly kites. Your attitude permeated my daily activities, making me stop to appreciate green blades of grass, a nest of peeping birds outside the window, and scampering squirrels feasting on nuts. At night, you showed me how stars glittered like diamonds, arranged into fantastic constellations that each contained a story. You know how to take the simple tasks of mothering and make them into the highest form of art.

The noblest calling in the world is that of mother. True motherhood is the most beautiful of all arts, the greatest of all professions.

David O. McKay

Whatever you do, whether in word or deed, do it all in the name of the Lord Jesus, giving thanks to God the Father through him.

Colossians 3:17 NIV

*Your homemade traditions have created
a unique source of happy memories.*

*I cherish the work of your hands that
added special creative touches to our home.*

As we approach a new holiday season, the mailbox is bombarded with catalogs. Store sales and decorations are a reminder that we must shop till we drop to make sure our twice-checked lists are completed in time. Yet when I look back over my favorite memories, I cherish our distinctive family traditions the most. You always trimmed the house with cheerful home-spun decor. The tree may not have graced the slick, glossy pages of a catalog, but it glowed with the light of homemade creativity. You pulled out favorite recipes and cooked them again and again. Your special cakes, some-times held together by toothpicks, always tasted sweetest when you let me help you bake them. With each change of season, you created new traditions that I'll never forget.

> Where we love is home, home that our feet may leave, but not our hearts.
>
> Oliver Wendell Holmes

Let the beauty of the LORD our God be upon us, and establish the work of our hands for us; yes, establish the work of our hands.

Psalm 90:17 NKJV

You've shown me that God is the source of all wisdom.

I'm blessed to have a mother who points me toward God's eternal wisdom found in the Bible.

In school I filled up my head with facts. I memorized how to multiply, spell words, and find cities on a map. I learned the words to songs and rhyming poetry. Yet none of these details made me a wise person. You taught me that wisdom comes from one source, as revealed through the Bible: God. I long to become a wise woman who makes the right choices at the right times. Sometimes I can be such a slow learner. When I hear a precept, I don't apply it right away. I wait until I go through an experience, often making a wrong decision. Then once again I return to truth. I'm thankful I never have to wonder how a person becomes wise. You remind me through your words and actions every day.

> If you've given your children to God, you've given them the best chance to succeed that you could ever give them!
>
> Michelle Medlock Adams

Oh, the depth of the riches both of the wisdom and knowledge of God! How unsearchable are His judgments and His ways past finding out!

Romans 11:33 NKJV

The legacy of your love continues
onward to future generations.

I know you are the one who will
always love me unconditionally.

Some people think it's important to pass on an inheritance of some sort, a legacy of material possessions. What you give to me is so much greater. You show me the true meaning of love, and not just in the big things. Your legacy comprises the thousands of little ways you show your love for me—the extra time you took helping me pick out new school supplies, cutting my sandwiches into triangles, reading to me even when you were tired, disciplining me when it wasn't fun for either of us, turning me toward the Father, teaching me how to laugh through my tears. You've given me so much, and now I have much to give as well. Thank you, Mom, for your legacy that continues forever.

Children and mothers never truly part—bound in the beating of each other's heart.

Charlotte Gray

The LORD your God . . . will keep his covenant and show his constant love to a thousand generations of those who love him and obey his commands.

Deuteronomy 7:9 GNT

*Your creativity has transformed many
a plain day into something special.*

*Your whole life is an act of service
to others.*

*You are an example of someone who culti-
vated the fruits of joy and peace in her life.*

Line by line, moment by moment, special times are
etched into our memories in the permanent ink of
everlasting love in our relationships.

Gloria Gaither

The memory of the righteous will be a blessing.

Proverbs 10:7 NIV